PAISLE

PAISLEY

By Rakhshan Rizwan

WITH AN INTRODUCTION BY
LEILA ABOULELA

THE EMMA PRESS

For Samee, Farzana and Rizwan

ℭ℞

THE EMMA PRESS

First published in Great Britain in 2017 by the Emma Press Ltd

ISBN 978-1-910139-78-3

A CIP catalogue record of this book
is available from the British Library.

Printed and bound in Great Britain
by Charlesworth Press, Wakefield.

The Emma Press
theemmapress.com
queries@theemmapress.com
Birmingham, UK

INTRODUCTION

We live in a time of relentless border crossing. Migration into Europe from Asia and Africa is not new but, as a subject, it has gathered urgency these past few years. In the news, there is one contentious story after another, the tone often strident and self-righteous. Poets, though, speak in a different way. They capture images, cadence and the swirl of thoughts in the mind. They understand that the country left behind has not really been left behind. It is still there, hovering, carried in the migrant's skin, infused in the family's memories and patterns of living.

For a poet, language comes first. But which language: the old or the new, the mother tongue or the one learnt at school? In *Partition,* language is learnt while still in the womb. While reading a letter from her mother, the 'unborn child kicks the quaint figures of speech and sucks the cloying Urdu with its small, webbed hands'. In *Speech Therapy,* the mother tongue was served 'with milk and warm skin'. The narrator contrasts this with the command to learn German and integrate – 'You prescribe your language to me like anti-depressants' – and describes its intrusion in the mouth as 'burning asphalt'.

And yet the new adopted country is not always to blame. In *Noon* there is reproach for those who had not prepared the narrator for her new life: 'My mother gave me this strange name— not to/punish—

European tongues— but/because it tasted sweet to her tongue—'. The duality of language is also expressed with skill and musicality in *Urdu/Hindi:* 'My voice is the mirror that breaks in Urdu,/in each piece, is the light of flowing Hindi'. Here the sadness and the rift is not between East and West but instead within the same country, adding poignancy and intimacy to this beautiful poem.

Can the migrant truly return to their roots? No doubt there is a change of perception, a greater distance. A barrier springs up, translucent perhaps, but still a barrier between the narrator and home. In *Dreamscapes*, the 'sun-stricken' city is observed through the window of an airplane, its 'blaring traffic diffused'. Through another window in *Lahore, by train,* the 'city becomes a fresco painted on fragile glass'. Already moving on, already having adopted a new home, the point of origin is left behind as it 'hurtles into linear time'.

Leila Aboulela
JULY 2017

CONTENTS

Lahore, by train

The city becomes a fresco painted on fragile glass:
past the slums, bone-carved children racing the train,
past identical yellow residences,
the parapeted houses of civil servants,
past sunburnt mosques in the skyline,
their domes the colour of dirty gold,
past the railway level crossing,
cows tied to poles and a makeshift masseur
palpating a man's temples, past the vegetable market,
burlap sacks piled high against a wall,
past vehicular bullies competing for primal dominance,
past the legless man dragging himself
with his bare hands against the gravel,
past enormous billboards with plump, fair-skinned families,
past the derelict beauty of the walled city, the narrow
streets and profusion of busy feet,
past shaded jharokas, precarious verandahs
with broken filigreed windows,
past the smoke rising from tukkatuk,
past the relentless rhythm of tortured meat,
past the lonely lanes of high walled mansions,
past the city's limits, gated communities with fences,
lined with brittle glass, past the pulse of privilege beating
like a steady heart, past the grey wasteland
of industry, blackened brick kilns, cement factories,
political jibes painted on the walls,
past fields ripe with lazy, yellow mustard,
past the sluggish Ravi, past the condensation
of breath on the window,
past the metallic scent of wet earth,

past the body soaking rain like a tea-leaf
immersed in flawless white porcelain,
Lahore gains momentum,
Lahore hurtles into linear time,
in all the windows, all the time,
its bone-broken bodies,
its red-brick walls,
its million souls
pass; for twenty years
the tired reel has run its
alternating sequence of
light. shadow. light.
and shadow,
on my face.

Partition

Her mother's letters arrive on yellowing papyrus from Lucknow and mimic the way she speaks: using the formal address *app* instead of *tum*. She lifts the affections, admonishments from the page and holds them close, smelling the black India ink and jasmine scent of her mother's hand; she sees the breaks in her train of thought, marked by blots of stray ink when she held the pen stationary. She washes down her mother's words of sandalwood and melancholy with warm tea. Her unborn child kicks the quaint figures of speech and sucks the cloying Urdu with its small, webbed hands. Honeyed phrases of an exiled language like savoury sweetmeats that a traveller brings back, wrapped in an oily newspaper, a little cold but still fragrant with a hint of saffron, a caress of cardamom, from across the border, from busy markets in Delhi, in Amritsar, in Ludhiana. Names, so familiar, of cities now invisible.

Speech Therapy

Put your language in my mouth like a cold strawberry
not a scythe.
Put your language in my mouth like crème brûlée
or a decadent macaroon,

put your language in my mouth
like parsley, not hemlock.

Put your language in my mouth the way my mother did,
serve it with milk and warm skin, not the way undertakers
inter carrion in the earth.

Put your language in my mouth,
a scented letter in a gold-rimmed envelope
or last season's roses pressed within the leaves
of a poetry book,

not like disinfectant meant to remove contaminants
from a crime scene.

I wish you had placed your language in my mouth
like a velvet glove, but instead you pour
burning asphalt onto my tongue, pave bitumen
and rock and flatness where there is none.

Learn German, you say, *integrate*.
I feel the reverberations of your language
like a line of freight trains through my mind.

You prescribe your language to me like anti-depressants,
to be consumed three times a day.

Buffet

We dine as if this meal
is our last, fat luqmas
of hot naan, newscasters
with husky voices,
stimulate our Pavlovian salivation,
we eat tragedy, morality, teenage
suicides, pillage, rape, the maddening
countryside of the mind
is overrun by this saccharine glaze,
of Pashtuns, Shias,
Hazaras, Balochis,
lower castes, Syrians,
Filipinos, cream-topped,
piping-hot, steaming-fresh
from the brazier, the red breaking news,
the familiar blurb which whets the appetite
and hits the spot each time,
but this gaping hole,
this will not fill, this canker sore,
we sit stirring the brew,
vapours of warm melted sugar rising,
we stir in the evening news,
and drown ourselves
in the tiny
teacups of our
collective conscience.

Colonial roses

There are ghosts of beech trees,
that lurk between chapters of history.
A host of white roses
feed on blades of sub-continental grass.

Here, pressed in the leaves of moth-eaten books,
see this crowd of golden daffodils?
Chapped like old lips, they collapse
into fine dust upon our fingers.
And that mighty sycamore tree,
which haunts the windows of my dreams,
its leaves rise and fall,
pure electricity pulsates down its tawny spine.
Fresh carnations grow in the mind,
in rows, with silver bells and cockle-shells,
planted along McLeod road –

But, neem leaves a deep scent
on the lines of my hand, henna patterns
curl in floral shapes over the fingers,
and from my palms, the whirling forms
of jasmine start to sprout, from silent bulbs
that lie beneath fields of blood.
The venous maps of the broken body
creep, intertwine, along a brick wall –
'Neem,' I whisper
to a phantom tree,
'Heal me,
of English roses.'

Urdu/Hindi

(after Agha Shahid Ali's 'Ghazal')

My voice is the mirror that breaks in Urdu,
in each piece, is the light of flowing Hindi,

My finger traces the edges of Urdu,
but always falters in the uneasy continent of Hindi,

My grandmother longed for a home in Urdu,
while she warmed her tea with leaves of Hindi,

I have cousins who learnt of life in Hindi,
but write letters to us in chaste Urdu,

Bahadur Shah cried in ghazals of Urdu,
his tears fell on cheeks of Hindi,

At Wagah, we watched the enemy in Hindi,
the hollowness of the heart is always Urdu,

Look, my mother said, this is where they bombed us in Hindi,
but I only see mortar shells of Urdu,

They fought these wars for the triumph of Urdu,
all the while, Noor Jehan sang only in Hindi,

The bride was sent off with promises of Urdu,
her gold jhoomar hung from her forehead like Hindi,

In my dreams, I remember the monsoon which fell in Urdu,
the smell of the soil bore traces of Hindi,

There are houses in andaroon Lahore that remember Hindi,
we erased their memories with whitewashed Urdu,

7

Their old owners haunt us in nightmares of Hindi,
we exorcise them with prayers of Urdu,

We apply henna on our hands in colours of Urdu,
the country bleeds in hues of Hindi,

What terrible times, the mothers are feeding in Hindi,
children that should be breastfed in Urdu,

Underage beggars beg for alms in Urdu,
their breath against the glass is Hindi,

Haye, the politicians are slitting our throats in Urdu,
while they sleep in feather beds of Hindi,

Exile is always experienced in shades of Urdu,
the stranger gazing at the vastness is Hindi,

I remember childhood in snatches of Hindi,
hibiscus grew in a shade deep as Urdu,

When Lahore spilled the blood of Urdu and Hindi,
Amrita Pritam wept for neither Urdu nor Hindi.

Balloon Wallah

Dangled in the air,
   helium-filled balloons,
  coloured outlines

The happy heads
   turn dark
   like bobble-headed ghosts

   Singing on strings, stretching their heads
  against a steel-scented wind

  Their owner looks up proudly
   at his shy, dark-faced children

He has not sold a single one
since June

Not a singlepenny to save
his soul

One day his
helium head
will
  e x p l o d e,
in the hot wind.

The Nawab's Daughter

She conjures a biryani out of turmeric fumes.
I had never touched the kitchen stove, she says,
holding out her hands,
they were so delicate, not made for rough work.
We used to recite Ghalib, Josh and Mir,
our cursive was calligraphy, not just mango orchards,
we were bequeathed whole villages upon marriage.
I saw your grandfather for the first time on the day we wed;
I did not gaze at him directly but caught his reflection
in a mirror and fainted;
fainting was customary and expected.
Her hands slice onions, cloves of garlic;
the monotonous staccato of chopped vegetables
resounds in the background
as she recites Ghalib, Josh and Mir,
we ate in silver plates and drank from silver cups
and rode on swaying palanquins, see my arms,
she says, pure Afghan blood.
We are princesses from Kabul, from Lucknow,
no man ever laid eyes on us. Unveiled,
she stirs salt into the rice and her
wounds and recites no more Ghalib, Josh or Mir.

Hair

Hair is erasing hair,
on our arms, our feet, even
our toes, or growing in wholesome
bunches in our ears, or the occasional rogue
hair that keeps protruding from our noses;
hair is picking at the fuzz on our upper lips,
hair is subduing hair
which bridges the gap between our brows;

but hair is also keeping hair,
and letting them grow wild and tangled,
hair is the promise
of hair crumpled and lovely,
in scarves like spring flowers
pressed between the leaves of a diary;
hair is massaging hair with almond oil,
the long, lean fingers of my grandmother
working her admonishments
into my scalp,
hair is never cutting long tresses,
hair is the sin of chopped hair;

hair is knowing which hair to keep
and which to lose; which to never show,
which to never cut and which to mercilessly slice;
hair is weeping at the loss of certain hair,
and certain terminal illnesses, but being glad
at the stifled growth of others;
hair is when to let them down
and when to hide them;
hair is memorizing all the rules of hair.

Women's Time

I pick out time like white hairs from between bunches
of black ones; time I stitch out of old clothes
and hand-me-downs; time I work into a tapestry,
from broken pieces of pottery; I piece together this time
from scraps and slivers; for me time is unfinished sentences,
poetry, the sun caught in shards of glass; for me time is
minutes tucked in between the slog, a pearl earring
falling out of a dusty drawer; time I find in my children's
shoes, between little soles and precious toes –

For you time is endless, a stretch.
For you time is a novel, the luxury of a plot.
For you time is sequential, the characters round.
For you time is a fragrant cup of tea, a midnight stroll.
For you time is an open window,
beckoning rows of forest and oak.

I want to carve a slice of your time for myself,
set alight your forest walks and your novels, smash those
smug bone china cups of simmering tea, rob you of your
ability to do things lingeringly, to saunter in street corners,
and be able to take in everything, the narrow alleys,
the overhanging jharokas, bougainvillea, also jasmine.

Eve

I collect bodies from the river, the misplaced smiles of acid-corroded faces, ajrak block-printed into foreheads and mouths. I carry looms of coiled ebony hair, hands manicured in textile factories. I bring with me the pawned bodies of aging actresses, the paisley motifs of child brides and the perfume-scented feet of call girls. I carry the burnt hair of beloved daughter-in-laws. I hold in my palm chiffon bruises, gota kinari lacerations. In my arms, I bear the porcelain legs of a divorcee, the painted cuticles of the unclaimed dumpster-child. I hold the henna-stained heads of women emancipated from love marriages with blows of silk to their skulls, their bones sliced open with peacock feathers and filled with a marrow of warm turmeric and fragrant jasmine. I carry the contorted limbs of trans women, caught in a Sufi whirl, their eyes glimmering with the festivities of Urs. I carry the voice of Benazir Bhutto, her particular English twang, the scent of musk and rose on her embalmed breath. I carry the rosy cheeks of Swati schoolgirls, their ruddy faces riddled with long-stemmed Persian roses and left to bleed an effervescent ark-e-gulab into their uniforms. I carry the bodies of the karo and the kari, decorated with gold leaf; their embossed forms become papier-mâché paintings. I carry the lace-trimmed wings of an underage rape victim. I carry the brittle ribs, the sacred latticework of an inner-city prostitute. I carry the deodar collarbones and polished shoulders of a brick kiln slave. I hold in my palms colourful vials of women's humiliation, their redolent tragedies. *Hurt them? We are the inheritors of Sufi poets, Moghul artisans. We worship women. It is these feminists who want to Westernize our women and destroy our happy families.*

Migrant

No one understands me
in this country
except
I.
Their patience with me
wears thin,
the length of a blade
of grass
in a field of snow.
The bank assigns me
a barcode,
and the immigration
office, an identification
pin.
I line my bills
in slim
files.
Eyes slant
when they see me,
lips are pursed.
Loyalties
of colour and race
are drawn
sharply.
In winter,
black tulips
fold their wings;

wind turbines
lacerate the air
with metal blades;
Leerdammer cheese
sits on a slice
of toast;
I
shed pounds
working two jobs,
in hopes of securing
a paper-thin
ticket home.

Dreamscapes

Airlifted a thousand feet,
you appear sun-stricken;
with your blaring traffic diffused,
your streetlights become glittering patches of colour,
embroidered like a pashmina shawl
which rests languidly
on your grey shoulders, now.

Then the scene wobbles, a grainy image
on an old television screen; it moves
out of focus; grey smog begins to envelop
the scene like a pool of amnesia.
Altitude, like a ticking clock,
times the beating of the great
Lahori heart, which begins to beat a little slower
with each passing moment.

The cartographer of time sketches
these maps of memory, fingers move feverishly
assembling history and stitching in street names,

but the pattern is lost forever.

As cold, packaged air is served
to comfort solitary travellers,
the city becomes an assortment
of hallucinations

to be treated with calming sedatives
of clinical food
served in small, bite-sized
portions.

Cordoba

There is history: one reads it in a book with silverfish.
There are evenings spent in the contemplation of history,
over a cup of jasmine tea, gazing at the Mezquita,
resplendent by night. In Hotel El Conquistador,
history is diminutive crusaders with crosses on their shields,
in window displays. History could take the form
of houses along cobbled streets, with wide-open courtyards
that gaze upon a dusky Spanish sky; houses that open
in corridors instead of rooms, to protect the zanana
from the eyes of intrusive outsiders. History is
oriental hamams with ornate facades and languid music,
in which white Europeans steam themselves.
But history also lies beneath the ground, it flows
in the subterranean layer of our consciousness –
It is in the way Spanish guards, with their trousers
drawn to their chests and their transceivers stuffed
in their back pockets, shake their heads,
their eyes blazing; it is the way they refuse to let you
remove your shoes, your socks, to acknowledge other histories
and usher you out; it is the roughness of their hands
against your skin, the firmness of their steps,
their discomfited faces, their clenched demeanour;
it is the graze of their blue eyes
against your brown ones; history is the fixed lines
on the conqueror's face.

Europe

They are digging the cities, not for gold,
but for origins. They have found,
beneath the brittle floors of Cordoba,
the remains of a Visigothic church.
And beneath the church is the Oracle of Delphi,
and beneath that a fisherman and a wishbone,
and underneath that, coils of the Dead Sea Scrolls
in the Aramaic language, which speak of floods
inundating the earth. And under that,
the menacing tail of a Chinese dragon
placed on the bodies of Muslim kings
wrapped in Mongolian carpets adorned with the boteh,
the paisley symbol soaked in royal blood.
They have found broken pieces of Chinese pottery
and recipes for embalming cats. Under that
they have found an enormous Buddhist stupa,
a monk still in the lotus position,
the seventh Sikh guru. They have found
the manuscripts of Aristotle,
the libraries of Baghdad and Alexandria,
the Roman Parthenon, a tower of Pisa
which doesn't lean, the degenerate paintings
of Picasso, and Indian diadems.

They are restoring *The Chess Players*,
the fasting Buddha, the mummified cats,
but they are getting the order wrong.
They are re-arranging the manuscripts,
burning the libraries; they are keeping
the unleaning tower, and Picasso's *Guernica*;
they are keeping the Parthenon and Aristotle,
but Europa on her bull is rounding up the Sikh gurus
and the Spanish Iberians and driving them
to the precipice of history.
They have taken paisley captive and retained the Kohinoor,
but nothing else. Europa's long, blonde hair
trails all over the cathedral.
She supervises the undigging, the constant
unexcavating.

Noon

My name has a noon ghunna at the end— a noon
without a dot— ں — a deep—
nasal sound that lives at the bottom
of Pakistani throats— Germans call me 'Rakhsha'—
They make the 'R' thick— and pasty— like غ—
and are confounded by the— ں — 'Is it silent?'
'No,' I tell them, 'it is half-silent.'— So their
mouths try it— but the half-silence of it
makes their tongues stumble—
I wonder which forgotten histories bequeathed
our mouths this strange sound—
which passing empires taught our tongues—
the shades of noon—
My Urdu-Persian name—
gets lodged in the throats of
immigration officers like a wish-bone,
centuries of residual histories— claw at their jaws— confusing
their inexperienced tongues, their
teeth click hastily around the noon— ں —
the unpronounceable parts of my mongrel
name— cloaked in an Anglo-Saxon 'n'— make them pause
for breath— My mother gave me this strange name— not to
punish— European tongues— but
because it tasted sweet to her tongue—
the way she says it— she twists 'Rakhshan' into
Rakhshu— her voice like velvet crème brûlée—
When she calls me, I remember that
my name was not always a criminal—

20

a confounding intonation to be
policed at a border-crossing— but was—
something soft— that purred— I was
someone's Mashuk— beloved— I still get letters in the mail—
addressed to Mr. Rakhshmann— a sort
of retribution— for the verbal gymnastics
I put authority figures through— Sometimes—
I do not correct them— pleased at the Germanness
of my name— I wonder
what it would be to glide through Europe
my skin, my scarf, my eyes,
my words, my jaw— untouched by
the gazes and whispered words— of white Europeans—
To be Rakhshmann— blonde— and blue—
and protected in a conch-shell of my whiteness—
to be untainted— by history—
(What is it about white skin which makes it
unable to carry history? And
what is it about mine, that makes it able to carry it?)
The shape of my mouth accommodates intermediate
sounds, words at the precipice of Anglo-Saxon sounds—
Sounds that have burnt their boats to Germanic languages?
Sounds whose precarious crossings—
across land and water— determine
the maps of my life— fragrant sounds like
مل— ma— bittersweet like judaiyaan—
separation.

Paisley

Her first cry was unpainted, her second paisley,
her body was velvet, cross-stitched on paisley,

Ozymandias desired a male heir, not paisley,
history is carved into marble busts, not paisleys,

they tried to straighten her out, little paisley,
for she always curled at the tip like paisley,

on Grecian urns and bas-reliefs, figures of paisley,
not walking the vulgar streets, sisters of paisley,

interred into the body of cashmere, delicate paisleys,
and then kept indoors, in a perfumed box, centuries of paisley,

in Lahori newspapers the stories of bloodied paisleys,
skulls cracked, limbs burnt, dishonourable paisley,

they unmade the daughter of Eve, quivering paisley,
with corrosive acid, the effaced body of paisley,

on the aquamarine Jhelum, the motif, unmistakably paisley,
her shalwar buoying to the surface, the supine body of paisley,

in her children's mouths lie morsels of paisley,
wedged between her husband's teeth, slivers of paisley,

Eve-teasers slant their eyes, the body of paisley,
their caresses and whispered words, naked paisley,

bronze men on horseback rode on invisible paisley,
empires constructed, cities won, on the bare bones of paisley,

my grandfather erected a citadel on splayed paisley,
and wrote his biography with alphabets of paisley,

some day this city will be mine, wrote Paisley,
but her child suckled her dry, brittle bones of paisley,

when they lead us to the slaughter, they wrap us in paisley,
so beware of fine promises, gold, amber, and paisley,

if a Sufi dervish stops mid-whirl, her body becomes paisley,
she hurtles to the floor, wings of gossamer and paisley,

I hope, from under the earth shuddering bulbs of paisley
will grow into your mind, delphiniums and paisleys,

in a new country, let us dream of different paisleys,
find other obsessions, besides the curvature of paisley

On running

In your clothes, the scent of aftershave, boardrooms and corporate plans; in your hands, expensive Parker pens that guide the petrol-scented breeze on the bodies of hundreds of bonded labourers building another flyover in the June heat; on their necks, the perfume and prayers of their mothers mounted on cheap amulets; in their pockets, paan-stained rupee bills, folded into their palms by their wives who cook gourmet meals for the village landlords, interring turmeric, cardamom and their skin into warm pockets of roti; in their begum sahab's clothes, promises of silks and paisley, of velvety pleats, delicate beadwork, gota kinari, ajrak borders and cream-coloured puffed sleeves; as they steam press these dreams, warm water seeps into the lines of their palms; they touch Persian roses, leaves of chinar; in these mysterious floral shapes the secrets of class, caste, race and qismet are encoded; somewhere in the folds of silken cloth and expensive embroidery, the chapped hands of an ex-con lie trapped, the former drug addict, who now works his mind into metal paisleys and gold sequins; his fingers trace but do not touch the expensive bodies which slip into prêt-à-porter bridal corsets; the breeze bears the slightest ache of sweet peas and old roses; it carries the aroma of halwa wafted into the street from the corner shop, the diesel scent of long-distance carriers shipping goods through the narrow arteries of the country; the air percolates on the skin of a bride in cream sequins with Bobbi Brown lips; the city moistens her forehead, teases her airconditioned skin; the city hangs in exquisite oil paints above her bed, a city she has only ever seen from a high-end eatery in the old city; someone sees her face pressed into the window of her car, the face of Paul Klee's angel as it hurtles towards folds of more chiffon, wretched paisley, manifold contortions of velvet and designer lawn; in the air the sacred sounds of Maghrib azan resonate; devotees pour into the mosque as the air fills with the smell of ittar, starched shalwar kurtas and wilted jasmine; the muezzin trills overhead, summoning the faithful with promises not of silk but of Closeness to the Beloved; so she rips out the glass beads from her clothes, the paisleys from her skin; her lips grow warm on sacred incantations; her body slackens; paisleys uncoil and become flat, unstriated; she peels gold shoes off her feet, letting porcelain touch hot clay; she draws the city close and with only half her breath, half her courage, she runs.

ACKNOWLEDGEMENTS

Many thanks to Leila Aboulela for introducing the pamphlet and to Moniza Alvi for writing a thoughtful review of it.

'Lahore, by train' and 'Hair' originally appeared in *aaduna*. 'Partition' first appeared in *Blue Lyra Review*.

'Speech Therapy' first appeared in *Yellow Chair Review* and was the winner of a Rock the Chair Poetry Challenge.

'Urdu/Hindi' and 'Buffet' were first published in *Postcolonial Text*. 'Dreamscapes' and 'Colonial roses' were first published in *Muse India*. 'Balloon Wallah' was my first poem to be published in a literary journal. It originally appeared in *Cerebration*.

'Cordoba' was the 2015 winner of the Judith Khan Memorial Poetry Prize, which is awarded annually by Desi Writers' Lounge. 'Europe' initially appeared in *Bird's Thumb*.

This pamphlet was lovingly edited and curated by poet and editor Rachel Piercey.

ABOUT THE POET

Rakhshan Rizwan was born in Lahore, Pakistan, and then moved to Germany to study Literature and New Media. She is currently a PhD candidate at the Department of Comparative Literature at Utrecht University and a Witteveen Memorial Research Fellow at Tilburg University in the Netherlands. In 2015 she won the Judith Khan Memorial Poetry Prize.

ABOUT THE EMMA PRESS

The Emma Press is an independent publisher dedicated to producing beautiful, thought-provoking books. It was founded in 2012 by Emma Wright in Winnersh, UK, and is now based in Birmingham. Having been shortlisted in both 2014 and 2015, the Emma Press won the Michael Marks Award for Poetry Pamphlet Publishers in 2016.

The Emma Press is passionate about making poetry welcoming and accessible. Sign up to the monthly Emma Press newsletter to hear about their events, publications and upcoming calls for submissions. Their books are available to buy online, as well as in bookshops.

theemmapress.com
emmavalleypress.blogspot.co.uk